THE SUICIDE'S SON

The Suicide's Son

JAMES ARTHUR

THE POETRY IMPRINT AT VÉHICULE PRESS

Published with the generous assistance of The Canada Council for
the Arts and the Canada Book Fund of the Department of
Canadian Heritage.

SIGNAL EDITIONS EDITOR: CARMINE STARNINO

Cover design: David Drummond
Photo of the author by Summer Greer
Set in Filosofia and Minion by Simon Garamond
Printed by Marquis Book Printing Inc.

Dépôt légal, Library and Archives Canada and the
Bibliothèque national du Québec, second trimester 2019.

LIBRARY AND ARCHIVES CANADA CATALOGUING IN PUBLICATION

Title: The suicide's son / James Arthur.

Names: Arthur, James, 1974- author.

Description: Poems.

Identifiers: Canadiana (print) 20189067551 | Canadiana (ebook)
2018906756X | ISBN 9781550655223

(softcover) | ISBN 9781550655285 (EPUB)

Classification: LCC PS8551.R885 S85 2019 | DDC C811/.6—DC23

Published by Véhicule Press, Montréal, Québec, Canada
www.vehiculepress.com

Distributed in Canada by LitDistCo
www.litdistco.ca

Distributed in the U.S. by Independent Publishers Group
www.ipgbook.com

Printed in Canada on FSC certified paper.

for Henry

CONTENTS

I

Effigy

Everyone knows
who we are supposed to be
but we look like ourself not a scarecrow

dancing on air above the riot square
pelted by bottles and stones
o little boy little girl
o wide-open fire

for us it is the finest most natural thing
to lean into the wind
and start burning

Frankenstein's Monster

I'm aging very slowly, because every part of me
is already dead. I spent years in the Arctic,
eating seal fat and things better left unnamed, but now
I've got money, and a condo on the West Side.
I smell like formaldehyde, my teeth are grimy,

my limbs mismatched, but I'm happy in this place
where I'm one more person with panache
and an ugly face. I eat well. I can walk the bridge
Hart Crane walked, or get drunk
and not conceal it. I'm not Boris Karloff, lurching
around, a mute—I hate that guy;
I get laid. Here, people suffer without believing

that every stranger should have to feel it.
The other day I walked from Cleopatra's Needle
to the far side of the Harlem Meer, thinking
about the Rockefeller Center, and the gigantic
armillary sphere balanced on the shoulders

of the Atlas statue there. My pants
are fitted. My beret advances everywhere
like a prow. My name isn't Frankenstein.
Frankenstein was my inventor.

Ode to the Heart

I know it's the brain, not you,
that loves, or fails to love.
You don't turn cold over time;
you don't grow fonder.

But if I needed reminding
of what I have in common
with the ibis or the snail,
the narwhal or the tiger,
I could slip my hand
inside my shirt and feel you
at my core, a clockwork fist
clenching and unclenching,
lumping out your truth,
survive, survive, survive.

These valentines that at best
approximate your form—
you're blind to them, and to
the star-crossed lovers who
only speak their lines
and die. You don't care
whether poems rhyme;
whether poets of yesteryear
used up the mountains
and trademarked the sea;
you're indifferent to poetry.

At times, mid-conversation,
I feel you inside me, poised
for flight—a prehistoric
bird, hungry to prey
and ravage. Other times
I think you're talking to me
from your cage, instructing me:
if I know what I'm doing,
I'm not doing it right.

Ode to an Encyclopedia

O hefty hardcover on the built-in shelf in my parents' living room,
O authority on linen paper, molted from your dustjacket,
Questing Beast of blue and gold, you were my companion

on beige afternoons that came slanting through the curtains
behind the rough upholstered chair. You knew how to trim a sail
and how the hornet builds a hive. You had a topographical map

of the mountain ranges on the far side of the moon
and could name the man who shot down the man
who murdered Jesse James. At forty, I tell myself

that boyhood was all enchantment: hanging around the railway,
getting plastered on cartoons; I see my best friend's father
marinating in a lawn chair, smiling at his son and me

from above a gin and tonic, or perched astride his roof
with carpentry nails and hammer, going at some problem
that kept resisting all his mending. O my tome, my paper brother,

my narrative without an ending, you had a diagram
of a cow broken down into the major cuts of beef,
and an image of the Trevi Fountain. The boarding house,

the church on the corner: all that stuff is gone.
In winter in Toronto, people say, a man goes outside
and shovels snow mostly so that his neighbors know

just how much snow he is displacing. I'm writing this
in Baltimore. For such a long time, the boy wants to grow up
and be at large, but posture becomes bearing;

bearing becomes shape. The man makes a choice
between two countries, believing all the while
that he will never have to choose.

Interpretation of a Painted Landscape

This little world is a quiet one. Cattle graze on a rock
jutting out above the bay, while sailboats,
brown and grey, grey and brown, drift above the harbor
like weather-beaten swans. One cow, standing at an angle
to the other members of the herd,

looks as if a strange thought had occurred to her
and almost immediately gone away. Who knows where
the boats are going, and whether the business
taking them there is wicked, or benign? Are the animals
to be loaded onto ships, and shuffled off to slaughter,
or have the cowherds brought the cattle here
simply for the pleasure of spending the morning
by the water? The only people we can see

are represented in profile, or from behind,
so we can't read their features, any more than we
can really know the mind of that solitary cow.

Everything is at the center, and
at the periphery: a landscape values people
at the level that it values other things.
Soon the great grey ships will unwind themselves
from their torpor, take the wind, and depart.
A pair of gulls are so remote, they might as well
be disembodied wings.

Children's Book

In which a newborn cricket walks across a field,
unable to reply to the greetings of the mantis, the moth,
and the dragonfly, until his rubbing of wing on wing

becomes a sound that can speak for him. When the last page turns,
the book itself makes a chirruping. Here is the church, and the steeple.
Here is the coffee table where the child lines up a squad

of plastic people. Can the child tell the difference
between himself and other things? He totters back and forth
on a tractor mounted on a spring. Here is the tension

of a string pulled tight, and the child's father rolling over and over
and over in the night: the cricket book, after much rough reading,
now chirrups on its own. Finally the father, knowing

what must be done, opens up the book with a sturdy paring knife,
looking for whatever little engine, whatever little part,
makes the life-like cricket sound. Here is the trailer, the baler,

the harrow, the plough. Can a stem grow up from inside a stone?
Here is how to sit in silence and be alone. Here's the yard
where yesterday the child sat watching as blowing branches

made and remade daggers of light and shade. The book's voice box,
to the father's eye, looks like a dime-sized bicycle bell,
and as he pries it free, the chirruping intensifies,

becoming something like the death cry of a creature
with an actual beating heart; something like a metal prong
banging indifferently on another metal part.

Goodnight Moon

I used to be as unsentimental as anyone could be.
Now I'm almost absurd, a clown, carrying you on my shoulders
around and around Palmer Square, through the cold night wind,
as stores lock up, and begin closing down.

Goodnight, fair trade coffee. Goodnight, Prada shoes.
Goodnight soon, my little son.
You're a toothy, two-foot-something sumo—a giddy, violent elf—
jabbing your finger at the moon,
which you've begun noticing in the last week or two. *Moom, moom*—
for you, the word ends with a mumming, as it begins.

For me, beginnings and endings
are getting hard to tell apart. There was another child
your mom and I conceived, who'd now be reading
and teaching you to read—who we threw away
when he or she was smaller than a watermelon seed.

The chairs; the domestic bears; the clocks; the socks;
the house—
once again a strange cow springs
from the green ground, beginning the enormous leap
that will carry her above the moon.

Hundred Acre Wood

Some of these stories are too sweet for me.
Winnie-the-Pooh is so innocent, his little songs leave me cold.

But I like this—your hand across my hand,
your head against my shoulder. Your first winter, I carried you

even along the margins of the highway,
strapped against my chest in a sling. *You never can tell with bees,*

says Pooh, who seems to believe that almost nothing can be told,
but I am your morose, restless father,

and you are four years old. You like front-end loaders
and every kind of train;

I like reading to rooms of strangers, and a few drinks at the airport
while I'm waiting for my plane.

I like the book's final chapter, a story you don't yet understand,
in which boy and bear

climb to Galleons Lap for one last look out across the land—
at the sandy pit, the six pines,

the Hundred Acre Wood. *Don't forget me*, says the boy to the bear,
who has no wish to understand

what he does not already know. Little boy who I carried
through the winter in northern Michigan,

I like hearing you in the morning
when you lie in your dark room, and sing.

School for Boys

I believe in the power of original sin,
in the wound
that keeps on wounding. The son
of the suicide
becomes a suicide. His own son
becomes a drunk. You're not meant
to be so unhappy,
you think, so it must be something
that you've done;
there must be a reason why you are
the way you are.

I've forgiven the teenage pedophile
who lived a few doors down
when I was seven.
The things he did to me
I'm sure were done to him at home.
Sunday afternoons, I'd be sent out
into the yard
where I could do no harm, beyond
decapitating
my mother's tulips, or torturing
the roly-polys
in the rotted-out retaining wall
around the flowerbed.

I and other boys would fight,
shoplift, or wreck each other's fortresses
of plywood boards
and brick. Or earn a nickel from the beer store
for every bottle that we found
in the no-man's-land of alleys that led
both north and south.

The anger, the shame:
over time, these things just become
a piece of who you are.
You build around them, since you can't
burn them down.
One boy, by far the most precocious forager
in our tribe, stole a box
of 3-D movie glasses
from the loading dock behind the Cineplex
and brought it to my parents' house
with the idea
that we'd sell the glasses pair by pair
at school, but the box sat below the deck,
going nowhere. In time
its contents were scattered and destroyed.

In time, I was sent to a private school dedicated
to forming the whole boy:
his body, his conscience, his character,
his mind.
There too some men did prey on children
in darkness
of a different kind. My fellow students

gave me
lessons on strength and weakness
that I will not forget.

And yet, many of the faculty—masters,
they were called—
were among the most decent men I've known.
One giant of a physics teacher
who sometimes
would grab boys by the collar
or roar into their faces, while gripping them
by the ear—
the man roamed the corridors scowling,
on a rolling cloud of fear—
brought me into his office,

and, after making me swear I'd never tell
another boy, opened a sketchpad
of watercolor paintings. They were his own:
the most fragile
lilies, snapdragons, and other flowers,
unfolding like translucent creatures
from the ocean floor.

He let me sit there in silence
turning pages for half an hour. *Life
is not a boys' school,*
he told me; *be one man for the world
and another for yourself.*
Then he put his paintings away
on a high shelf.

When I was seven, all that
lay far ahead. In my Grade Two class
there was a pale, elfin redhead,
I won't say his name,
whose mother always sent him to school
in a tie and blazer.
How many times we made that boy cry
I just don't remember.
He said he was an extraterrestrial
in disguise, that his people
would soon arrive and kill us, every one,
or take us off
to be vivisected. And his story didn't change
when we threw his books

into the trash. Or when we pinned him
to the ground
and made him eat the dirty snow.
I think I half-believed him.
But his people never came.

Darth Vader

This battle station
has no ping pong, and no décor—only consoles, catwalks,

a reactor core. You are angry all the time. You've always been
an angry man.

Fuck the innocent people of Alderaan. Give in to your anger.
Give in to your hate.

You need more subordinates to asphyxiate.
Your task, this morning—

standing at the window, staring into outer space. Your face
is a mask. There is a mask

underneath your mask, underneath your mask,
underneath your face.

To Geoffrey Chaucer

I wish I could get your advice
on how to write this second book. I give myself directives
to stay on the subject, to expand,
but the words clot into jelly, or just will not be
whistled up at my command.

Translator, astronomer, courtier, diplomat,
you were a renaissance man
before the Renaissance was a thing. I teach creative writing
and am a monoglot.
All the books that I should've read in college and did not
beam out to me from my bookshelves
their chorus of reproach.

Reading you, however,
was fun from the start, overhearing your pilgrims
trading stories to pass the time, at a decasyllabic canter
in your trademark riding rhyme.
Even if those first pages of Middle English
each took an hour to decode,
your big book, like a wise, old, wicked lover, devoured me
in my dorm room,
cover to cover. You saw pretension everywhere
and liked people more for it, not only nonetheless.
You taught me that underneath the fig leaf, there is a place in art
for pubic hair, for sweat,
for twelve greedy friars dividing up a fart.

Today, instead of selling fake indulgences, the pardoner might be
a life coach or a psychiatrist.
I like to think the wife of Bath would be tenured somewhere,
teaching English Lit.
Is your gracious knight, for all his handsome speech,
meant to be a bore?
Is the prioress
an anti-Semite who feels compassion only for her dogs? Your ironies
hide inside other ironies,
making you difficult to pin down;
you gave yourself a place among the pilgrims, and made yourself
a chump, who believes whatever he is told
and wants above all to be liked.

I wish you'd come visit me in one of those dream visions
that were always happening
to poets of your time, and guide me through the grey neighborhoods
of the underworld
or to the feast of St. Valentine, and teach me to bring life's largeness
to the page.

And I wish I knew exactly what you meant
by that note
that's tacked like a kick-me sign onto the back end
of your book,
the coda where you take back half the stories that you've told,
retracting *many a song*
and many a lecherous lay because you're sorry, you say,
for mixing up the godly
and the sexy, the naughty and the good. Is this remorseful one
Chaucer the pilgrim,

full of religious feeling at his long journey's end?
Or is it you
yourself, on your own deathbed, afraid of Hell,
because you could not spin your gold
back into straw, or de-alchemize it into lead?

It's cold this morning in Rodgers Forge.
A new gas line going in
has brought men, jackhammers, heavy trucks. The lead man
whistles on and off
throughout the day, while unperturbed, a few dry leaves
turn and whirl, tornado-style,

as though inside the rim of a bowl of air. *Love life more;*
love life more—
I string and restring
my one phrase, trying to build a home inside it,
whereas you are a great river, bringing news
from countless towns
and jurisdictions, places that are familiar
but unknown.

Wind

        it's true sometimes I cannot
stop myself from spilling
      the recycling

unpetalling apple blossoms
          raiding a picnic
making off with napkins I'm nothing
      until I happen
flipping an umbrella outside-in
           throwing its owner
      into a fumble
pelting the avenue with sleet or dust

at times downtown
      riding over galleries of air
so full of high excitement howling
I borrow an old woman's hat
        and fling it into the road

arriving with news of the larkspur
        and the bumblebee
at times embracing you so lightly
in ways you don't even think of
      as touch

Fixer-Upper

We hire guys who drywall, paint, and spackle.
We hire guys who arrive in hazmat suits to pry up the asbestos.
Inside the air-con ducts, there's a decade's worth of dander;
the duct guys snake a hose, wide as a tree, up the south wall,
through a window, and screw it to a ceiling vent. *Poof*—
outside, in the yard, a three-story grime cloud scatters.

The men who come to clean the gutters
find dead squirrels, dead birds, packed inside the rotting sod
like a clan of dolls in one cradle. Elsewhere, plastic saints,
ceramic shamrocks, stacks of old clothes, a rocking horse,
a walking stick—all left behind. We get rid of it. The ragged rosebushes
we dig up, and pile curbside. Clearing away rancid leaves
and a knee-deep riot of creeping vines, we find a phone,
a ring of keys, and, buried upright under coarse, tough weeds,
a lawn sign from a long-lost presidential campaign.

What seems irreplaceable, we set aside,
in case the previous owner ever does call back. Poking around
in the overgrown grass, we find a hunk of cement,
embedded with irregular bits of colored glass
arranged around a pair of hand-prints, small and big.

The girl's bedroom is now where our son sleeps.
He rolls his fire engines across the windowsill.
Opening a closet door, we find, written inside,
in felt-tip pen, in a child's hand,
This is the O'Malleys' house.
The O'Malleys lived here.

I Hear the Voices, and I Read the Front Page, and I Know the Speculation. But I'm the Decider, and I Decide What Is Best.

after a statement by George W. Bush

I know how to use a washing machine.
I know the three small figures crossing a stone bridge
on my wife's and my Blue Willow plates.
The university is bounded by fences with iron gates.

I know the pleasure of undressing someone,
of being undressed. I can clean a nosebleed
from a pillowcase, or a slosh of coffee from a sleeve.
I'm no good at deciding, but I hear the voices
and I read the front page.
I know the feeling of wanting to be buried
with your concubines.

Moment by moment, you make your life;
your life gets made. A man I know
once caught a carving knife that was dropping
from a kitchen counter. Instantly—
with no thought of danger—he reached out
and wrapped his fingers
around the falling blade.

Drone

I am the drone of a banjo's fifth string.
I am the drone that gives bottom
to the chanter in a highland fling.

Haw, hum. I am the drone of drone itself,
planted so pleasurably in the mouth.
A monotone. A lodestone. I'm an MQ-9,

a Reaper Drone, ranging wide, circling
in the sky. No windows, no cockpit.
No one onboard. See how my Hellfires

fly faster than sound. I am drone,
from the tymbal under the cicada's wing.
I gather no pollen, and have no sting.

Arriving unheard, I haunt the sky
and inseminate the queen before I die.
I am a poetry that celebrates power.

I bring. I bring. The white house
is empty. I bomb air. I bomb breath.
My country, 'tis of thee I sing.

II

A Local History

My grandmother's house was always full of flies.
They'd crawl across each other on the windowsill
or would be spinning out their noisy dying

everywhere, in such number, you could sweep forever
and not get all the dead flies off the floor. Out of the house
and downhill, in a marsh of cattails and bristle-sided reeds,
milkweed pods kept cracking open, leaking seed across the air,
renewing the existence of their species
in the way they'd done from year to year.

Way back when, some hard-handed Methodist pioneer
had somehow wrenched up every stone
big enough to break a plough,
and piled them all throughout the woods,
where they still were, in mounds, when I was growing up:
like barrows heaped above the decomposed remains
of the violent Saxon kings, whose grave-goods
featured large in my imagination.

My grandmother's gone. Before she died, she lost her words,
her house, her name, but for me, she's still a hard old woman
walking downhill at dawn, long into autumn,
to skinny-dip in her weed-choked, freezing pond.
A hedge of wind, a wall of suburban snow—
my father's father's ashes are in the ground
in southern Ontario. Something I read in college
and for whatever reason have not forgotten

is that the Saxon barrow-makers,
living among the wrecks of Roman buildings
they could not copy
or restore, saw themselves as late arrivers, as an *after-folk*
living on the graves of a greater folk
who'd gone before. *Where is the horse, where the rider,*
some now-nameless Saxon wrote,
grieving for a people who his own forebears
had annihilated, assimilated,
or driven into the sea.

In a Rented Cabin in the Haliburton Highlands, Oriented Toward Algonquin Park

Everything is grimy and in disrepair.
The curtains are smoke-damaged, the wallpaper half-unglued.
The kitchen probably looks as it did
when the cabin was built, in 1962. The sliding door gets stuck.

But out front, the Muskoka chairs planted in the sand
seem to be paying close attention to the lake, as if bound by some power
to contemplate this one landscape
until they know it to its core: perfect watchers, scorning nothing,
absorbing all existence exactly as they should,
so they register every little deepening of the soupy summer dark,
and the grey curl
that's slipped free of Mrs. McKechnie's bathing cap.

Ice once covered all this shield rock—for a hundred miles around—
before melting back, leaving raw granite
and these lakes. As night comes on, a kayak crawling in the dark
looks not like any physical object
but like something more abstract gliding on the surface
of the open water's mind.

Wolf

No costume, Red Riding Hood, ever could disguise
this jaw, this brush-like tail, this tongue.

By now you must be married to a woodcutter
or to a woodcutter's son
but I am still entangled in the forest of your hair. Come back;
strip of this nightgown, and I'll show you
how to raid a chicken coop,
how to step around a snare.

Only stroke my face again
as if it were one of the remaining wild places of the world.
Does it make me a donkey, eating shards of apple from your hand?
I'd devour every grandmother in the world
to get back into your basket. Look at the savage brambles
pasted through my fur. Don't tell me that my enormous teeth
don't frighten you anymore.
My enemy the moon looks down at me like a cauterized eye
as I creep into the village

and softly call your name. Little scholar, little flame,
shy girl in a crimson cowl, let me unfasten the buttons
that you've done up to your collar.
The shepherd's boy keeps crying wolf
because he thinks we'll never come. Red Riding Hood,
come help me blow these houses down.

It's not like I'm not able
to live inside the law. It just makes me crazy,
seeing little pigs building up their houses
with hickory sticks and straw.

Renaissance Fair

But not so much the Renaissance as the Middle Ages;
not so much the Middle Ages as the Olden Times.
Baronets and ladies walk the streets of this mock medieval village,
mingling with wizards and with Viking raiders.
A druid in the coffee line is eating a bag of deep-fried pickles.

Now come the horses for the joust, hung with colors, prancing!
Now come the knights—some, long of tooth
and sitting heavy in the saddle, but knights anyway,
equal parts gentleness and power. This is Camelot at its apogee,
where chivalry is figured as a flower;
the knights spur forward, into a theater of battle.

But Camelot would not be Camelot
were it not unsound
in some way that no enchantment could ever mend.

Alas! for all the pageantry that must eventually
stutter to an end: for the Scotch eggs
and the crab cakes, and the slow-roasted mutton shoulder.
Alas! for the beer tent, and the dads in chainmail
pushing their kids uphill in strollers
to cars and SUVs
waiting to carry their owners back, past gas stations
and off-ramps, to jobs in Baltimore and DC
or over the Chesapeake Bay Bridge

to the pretty little towns that dot the Eastern Shore.
Eight weeks of the year, the Renaissance is here;
there's really nothing much for the other forty-four.
Camelot is what you feel nostalgic for
even before it fades.

Nostalgia

The museum was closed, so no one saw
the statue of Adam
tumble to the floor, and break. No one saw
the plywood pedestal
collapsing, when it couldn't hold the marble man
one second more.
Cameras weren't allowed at the scene of the accident
so no public images exist
of the curators sifting
through every fragment, hoping to rebuild Adam
from the wreck, but you can imagine
the disconnected hand
still gripping the apple. You can imagine the head
broken off at the neck.

*

There's no going back to the garden, she said—
no more reading poetry
in the reservoir park. No more origami.
There won't be any more lunches at the Green Room
or long weekends in New York.
No travelling by ocean liner.
No silk stockings, no poke bonnets, or broadfall pants
for the men.
No collecting beach glass
or writing out letters by fountain pen.

As the man and woman walked deeper into exile
from the garden outside of time,
their memories of where they'd come from
grew hazy, and recombined,

becoming pieces of a magic jigsaw
that never would stay together
or make any picture twice—
now a mystic wilderness
where a hyena was licking the injured flank
of a giraffe; now a couple
courting in the foreground of an ancient cenotaph.
The lovers had invented nakedness
and put on their garments made of shame.
The children
weren't children any longer, and everything

had changed—except for the angel
whose particular job it was
to stand at the garden gate forever, making sure
the man and woman
did not reenter, if somehow they came back.
And because angels
don't mind laboring without reward, the angel
didn't feel bored or disenchanted;
he didn't spend eternity on the thought
that he was getting punished
because of something that somebody else had done.

Whether he represented stubbornness
or human consciousness
or just himself, or the sun, he kept watching
all directions,
all at once. And never for a moment
did he put down his burning sword.

Model-Train Display at Christmas in
a Shopping Mall Food Court

These kids watching so intently
on every side of the display
must love the feeling of being gigantic:
of having a giant's power
over this little world of snow, where buttons
lift and lower
the railway crossing gate, or switch the track,
or make the bent wire topped with a toy helicopter
turn and turn
like a sped-up sunflower. A steam engine
draws coal tender, passenger cars, and a gleaming caboose
out from the mountain tunnel,
through a forest of spruce and pine, over the trestle bridge,
to come down near the old silver mine.

Maybe all Christmases
are haunted by Christmases long gone:
old songs, old customs, people who loved you
and have died. Within a family
sometimes even the smallest disagreements
can turn, and grow unkind.

The train's imaginary passengers,
looking outward from inside,
are steaming toward the one town they could be going to,
the town they have just left,

where everything is local
and nothing is to scale. One church, one skating rink,
one place to buy a saw.
A single hook-and-ladder truck
and one officer of the law. Maybe in another valley
it's early spring
and the thick air is redolent of chimney-smoke and rain,
but here the diner's always open
so you can always get a meal. Or go down to the drive-in
looking for a fight, or stay up
all night, so tormented by desire, you can hardly think.

Beyond the edges of the model train display, the food court
is abuzz. Gingerbread and candy canes
surround a blow mold Virgin Mary, illuminated from within;
a grapevine reindeer
has been hung with sticks of cinnamon. One by one, kids
get pulled away
from the model trains: Christmas Eve is bearing down
and many chores remain undone.

But for every child who leaves, another child appears.
The great pagan pine
catches and throws back wave on wave of light
like a king-sized chandelier, announcing
that the jingle hop has begun,
and the drummer boy
still has nothing to offer the son of God
but the sound of one small drum.

Tree-Planting

The crew come from all over, because the money is that good.
      Women, men—
many are students planting as a summer job, moiling in the mud,
      sweating bug spray.
One day off, four on, in cut-offs above long johns, a bag of saplings
      on each hip.
As one hand does the spading, the other slides
      a pine plug
into the ground. One breath, one stride, and the smack of shovel
      cutting clay. Some highballers
who've been coming since before the crew bosses were on the crew
      are old-timers
at thirty-five, masters of the trade, who've customized their shovels
      by cutting inches
off the shaft, or by grinding a kicker off the blade. One planter,
      famous for having duct-taped
his fingers to the handle of his spade, tells the story again, deadpan—
      It's not so easy
to wipe your ass when you've taped a shovel to your hand. Nights off,
      planters pile into trucks
for the long drive into town: for hot showers and the bar.
      There are fights:
some regulars are sick to death of kids with nose-rings, mohawks,
      and money to throw around.
One planter's doing a Philosophy Ph.D. One guy stays up all night
      getting drunk
on a chair in the river. And there's a new guy who no one else can stand.
      His crewboss

is *against* him, he says—*fuck her* for giving him another bullshit
        piece of land.
He has no tent, but beds down in a rusted-out sedan
        with an ex-fighting dog
that wants to kill every other dog in camp. Always keep your head down,
        getting off a helicopter,
and always walk downhill. Always wash off the trucks before going into tow
        Don't plant shallow.
Don't plant deep. Sometime between contracts, the planter with the dog
        vanishes
and never does come back—fired, everyone assumes, until a story gets arou
        about the man and dog
walking out into a field with a softball and a bat, to play the game
        they always played:
the man would crack a high long shot for the bleachers, and the dog
        would run it down,
except this one time, when the man somehow timed it wrong. As he begar
        his downswing
the dog sprang into the air, jaws open, catching the ball, and the full force
        of the bat coming down:
the dog lived. The dog died. The outcome is unclear. —Let's go back
        to the field, with the leap
still inside the dog, the blow still unstruck. Man and dog are happy,
        each in the company
of a creature he truly loves—so let's leave them as they are,
        in the field.
Quiet. No breeze. The red stitching on the softball
        hanging in the air.

In Al Purdy's House

It is strange, living in the house
of a writer who has died. I use your cutlery,
your typewriter. I read your autobiography
while lying in your bed, trying to imagine Roblin Lake
and this lakeside piece of land
as they were sixty years ago, when you and Eurithe
built the A-frame by hand,
with no experience of carpentry, using salvaged lumber
and whatever materials you could find.

Critics seem to always talk you up or talk you down,
casting you as the forerunner
of all Canadian poets who were to follow,
or else as a roughneck and a clown.
For me, it's enough that you were many times demoted
during a war you found unreal;
that you lived and wrote according to an image
you had in mind;
that you called your house *A drum for the north wind,
a kind of knot in time.*

Your mother's good china
is still here, asleep inside the hutch. History,
your personal history, hangs around the record player,
which I haven't dared to touch—
but this year there's been so much rain,
Roblin Lake has climbed up fifteen feet on the grass,
making an island of the short peninsula
you and Eurithe added to the shore.

Standing at the window near the kitchen,
watching a single sailboat pass
back and forth across a distance
that couldn't be more than a mile from end to end,
I feel a collapse of distinctions
between the real and the unreal,
between what has already
taken place, and what is happening right now,
as if time had been doubled over into itself,
like a sheet of folded steel.
Cottage country becomes backcountry,
as houses along the shoreline
blink out and disappear.

I know better than to make myself at home
in a house that isn't mine.
Soon, I'll leave the keys
on the counter, turn the lock
on the inside, step out, and close the door.

Maybe because I'm left-handed
I made my way through your collected poems
back to front,
so I ended with the love songs of a young man—
poems for women
you seduced, or thought you might seduce—
and I began
with your regrets, the many places you visited,
and your elegies for friends
who during my backward progress
came to life one by one.

III

On the Move

Now that my work's done and it's Saturday,
now that my young son is out somewhere
with his mom, I might as well roam all morning,
spying on the filthy squirrels, and on the shapes
that disintegrating leaves have painted on the sidewalk.
I might as well spend the morning talking to myself,
hoping for meaning and unmeaning to braid
and begin teaching me what to say.

Some days I feel like a monarch at wing, meandering,
not really deciding where I go—
as programmed as the stubborn birds
building nests of twigs and spit. Each bird pipes the song
that it was taught, and transmits the song
to its own offspring.
Earthworms, driven up by last night's rain, have squirmed
onto the asphalt to slowly fry.
I save some, who glue and wriggle,
but there are just so many. They almost seem to want to die.

Day by day, I'm feeling my way into fatherhood,
learning what my son is to me, and I to him;
my boy, my kid, an eight-toothed homunculus
clutching an acorn in his fist, bewildered
that a paper plate set down in the grass on a windy day
won't stay put, but lofts, and spins away.

By the time I'm downtown, I'm turning back,
in thought, if not yet with my feet.
Before I'm back on my own street,
I'll have twice walked by the little wedge of ground
where people of this neighborhood
bury their dead dogs and cats. A rawhide bone;
a ball of yarn, water-logged by the frowsy rain.
Animals have never meant very much to me,
but I've got them on the brain these days—

how magnetic navigation brings spawning salmon home;
how predation, variation,
and the winnowing-down of things gave shape
to a world of species, giving them gills, wings,
and feet. But I'd rather be dead than be a creature
of any other kind. I walk upright, practicing
the song of my species, by speaking.

At Hearst Castle

Fifty-eight bedrooms. Forty-one fireplaces.
On the upper terrace
is a copy of Canova's statue of the Graces
wrapped around each other
in a three-way caress, wearing only enough to emphasize
their casual nakedness. Our tour guide
talks about Hearst in the present tense,
as if he were alive. "Hearst," says our guide, "sits here
every morning, with his paper …
Hearst loves to be outside."

Most of the castle
is reinforced concrete. We see the Spanish minaret
and the New Kingdom Sekhmet statue
that's been defaced by the rain.
We see the Mexican fan palms
and the English tapestries. We ourselves are the only
uncurated element of the scene,
in T-shirts and sunglasses,
taking pictures with our phones, doing what we can
to keep each other out of frame.

We see the sun snagged in the branches
of a glistening orange tree
like one colossal fruit, or a single burning flower,
or a message from Management
reminding us that our tour will be wrapping up
in approximately half an hour.

Barbed wire in the form of painted thorns
encloses a painted Sacred Heart.
One of these statues
once belonged to Napoleon Bonaparte. Here
is human history
with all context sheared away, as if
there were no context, or as if the context
had been destroyed. As if no context
were the context, and the only context
there could be.
The road runs north to Ragged Point,
and on to Monterey.

Ararat

did it really happen
the way I remember
before the rupture

and the flood before
I sent out the raven
and the dove

and my family and I
came down the mountain
into a country

we couldn't recognize
did I really go out
and gather two animals

of every kind
I hear them breathing
across the yarrow field

beasts with tapered quills
and ears drawn back
with brightly colored

scales and feathers
stranglers moving
without a sound

how many generations
have I now seen
descend from me

and multiply
I can't remember
who is which person's

son or daughter
but I remember
the two rabbits we saved

and the many more
we kept alive
just for slaughter

the animals
start screaming
the boat begins to rise

I gather wildflowers
from the valley
to please my little bride

am I nothing
but another creature
of the field

am I not in the mold
of the one who made me
why he would save me

from the water
and let me drown
in time in the shadow

of my ship that was
my church my home
that was my barn

The Death of Captain America

Cap will be buried in his costume, in his half-mask,
with his bulletproof shield of blue, red, and white,
and the Invincible Iron Man is inconsolable,
now that Captain America is dead.

If the man inside the coffin was a symbol, what ideals
did he represent? Did he believe in the right to bear arms,
or in big government? Was he disfigured from battle?
Did he have a schoolboy's face?
For some, he was an authoritarian endowed with physical grace,
but this morning even the paparazzi
seem moved by the manly grief of the mighty Thor.
What will become of the Pax Americana
now that Captain America is dead?

If he stormed the beach at Normandy
was he in the shadows at the hanging of Saddam Hussein?
Cap's enemy the Kingpin is here,
leaning on a diamond-encrusted cane.
Cap never drank, never smoked, was straight
as a bug-collector's pin,
but many a crooked man will walk a crooked mile
now that Captain America is dead.

The escalator's been broken since August.
The drinking fountain is full of cement.
Will the train stations descend into ruin
now that Captain America is dead?

Some people want a moral. Some, only a refrain.
Some want to go on injuring themselves
in the way they have
time and again,
but who will speak for the man inside the coffin—
his love of slapstick, his wide-open grin?
Will anyone speak of the man himself,
remembering what was best and worst in him?

Into the ground, the indestructible shield,
the myth, the one-man legion. Into the ground,
the man, the boy, and every toy or comic book
that ever pleased him. Into the ground.
Into the ground. Into the ground.
Captain America is dead.

Eloquence

I too have been to Blarney
and done the thing,
the kiss. With a line of other paid-up kissers behind me,
each waiting
for a turn, I leaned out backward from the castle parapet
into nothingness:
one touch of lips to stone, they say, and you'll be eloquent
all your life.

My eyes were shut, so I didn't see the upside-down abyss
between me and the world below,
or small figures on the ground, or any garden archipelago
of green …
but clutching the iron safety bar, I brought my mouth
to that damp stone,
whose country roughness had been rubbed away by lips
of every shape
and hue and tone. I want things from poetry

that it could never give:
power to undo, to mend. To compel forgiveness
and forgive. I know
kissing the Blarney Stone is just a thing to do
to say you've done,
but I thought, Give me
a silver tongue. Reader, if you're there, help me

play the fool
without becoming one, so I can be something more
than a lover from afar;
something more than a small-town mayor
in a dictator's tie;
something more than a centaur at the wedding feast
with a horse's heart
thumping a few feet below
his human one.

Leper Colony Seen from the Shore

At a certain bend on a barren stretch of coast,
there's a chapel made of stone.
All around are thorns. Inside, grey-faced icons
bless all the fingerprints and ash.
A pocketknife lies in the offering box,
along with prayers and coins.

The chapel door looks out to an island,
once a quarantine, close enough to be seen
on both stormy and sunny days.
Young men and women swim to it
or they cross in fishermen's boats;
there's not much to show
what the island was, not so long ago.

Troy

The war is wrapping up, and there's nothing left of Troy.
Broken stone; broken clay; a smoke-stain on the sky;
the Greeks even broke the skull and back of Hector's little boy.
Odysseus, packing up his bags, thinks, Soon I'll be home.

But this afternoon belongs to Ajax, son of Telamon,
standing by a flock of sheep he's butchered in a rage,
and like a man who's just shot up a shopping mall
or a school bus, or a bank, Ajax can answer all this killing
only with the killing of himself.
Soon he'll sit down and start to weep, like a naughty child
full of shame, because he is a man-killer
and a man-killer does not kill sheep.

The Greeks didn't come to halt a genocide
or to spread democracy. Behind their great encampment
are their island kingdoms, speckled against the sea.
Beyond, scavenged by turning seabirds,
are the Pillars of Hercules, said to bear the words,
"There is nothing beyond this point."

Study

no beast of theory
nor mere poet's creature
roaming the brain's
savannah eating words no
this is a real
giraffe an American
giraffe at the zoo
two kids stare its hoof pecks
the ground
like the heel of a walking
stick it slow steps
around the yard a living
crane whisking
its tail it shifts
and leans eating the leaves
hoisting its precarious
head before sailing
past the gate eyeing the
trucks what is going
on in its mind

On a Marble Portrait Bust in Worcester, Massachusetts

Someone with a careful hand
carved your center-parted hair,
which frames your forehead like a proscenium
and tumbles into ringlets
in front of either ear,

but we don't know the sculptor's name
or whose face
you represent, only that you were found
in the basement of a Spanish drugstore
in New York.

Classical in your proportions,
with a long, narrow nose,
you look out, pupilless, from your three quarter pose,
smiling as if to imply
that all questions of form are superfluous
and absurd. How fitting
that in your case the medium was subtracted,
not applied to a canvas
or built up word by word. Compact like a star,

with one long braid
bound behind your head. Cold, like a gun.
More absolutely pale
than any bone or shell, and your strict
hard surface sparkles in the sun.

Roar

The storm that howled all night has spun off east
and the blown-down leaves, mounded deep, are drying—

so employees of the city are out cleaning up, with leaf-blowers,
        stirring up a roar so big, their earmuffs can't block it,
only blend it—

        so the men hear the shouting of engine above engine
as a sound that's vague and far away, like the empty noise
        that children find in the cornet shells
that sea snails form, and leave behind. The leaves, lifted high, fly
        to a canary-colored truck

that's retrofitted with a heavy hose. —A diesel elephant
        with a cocaine nose, drawing
whatever comes near, sucking it in. Inside, the leaves

grind down to dust. But flying there, they're so
        delicate. Dragonflies, butterflies. They
        skitter across the air—

ACKNOWLEDGEMENTS

Versions of these poems first appeared in the following publications:

32 Poems: "At Hearst Castle"
Alaska Quarterly Review: "An Interrogator," "Effigy"
American Poetry Review: "Ararat," "In Al Purdy's House," "Wolf"
Hazlitt: "A Local History"
The Hopkins Review: "Fixer-Upper"
Horsethief: "Darth Vader," "Eloquence"
Little Star: "Frankenstein's Monster," "Roar," "On the Move"
Literary Matters: "To Geoffrey Chaucer"
The London Review of Books: "Tree-Planting"
Narrative: "Interpretation of a Painted Landscape," "Renaissance Fair," "Troy"
The New York Review of Books: "Children's Book," "Drone"
Poetry Northwest: "Ode to the Heart"
The Southern Review: "Hundred Acre Wood," Leper Colony Seen from the Shore," "Model-Train Display at Christmas in a Shopping Mall Food Court," "School for Boys"
The Walrus: "In a Rented Cabin in the Haliburton Highlands Oriented toward Algonquin Park"
The Yale Review: "Nostalgia"

"Goodnight Moon," "Ode to an Encyclopedia," and "Wind" were published in the Academy of American Poets' Poem-A-Day Project.

"The Death of Captain America" first appeared in *Resistance, Rebellion, Life: 50 Poems Now* (Knopf 2017), and "I Hear the Voices, and I Read the Front Page, and I Know the Speculation. But I'm the Decider, and I Decide What is Best" was published in *Still Life with Poem: 100 Natures Mortes in Verse* (Literary House Press 2016).

"A Local History" was reprinted in *The Best of Canadian Poetry 2016* (Tightrope Books 2016) and also in *The Next Wave: An Anthology of 21st Century Canadian Poetry* (Palimpsest Press 2018). "In Al Purdy's House" was anthologized in *Beyond Forgetting* (Harbour Publishing 2018), "Wind" in *HERE: Poems for the Planet* (Copper Canyon Press 2019), and "The Death of Captain America," "Drone," and "A Local History" in *Resisting Canada: An Anthology of Poetry* (Véhicule Press 2019).

"Drone" was reprinted in *The Drum*, and "Fixer-Upper" on *Poetry Daily*. Anstruther Press brought together some of these poems in the chapbook *Hundred Acre Wood*.

I am very grateful to the following organizations for their support: the Al Purdy A-frame Association, the American Antiquarian Society, the Amy Clampitt Fund, the Anderson Center for Interdisciplinary Studies, the Berkshire Taconic Community Foundation, the Bread Loaf Writers' Conference, the Canada Council for the Arts, the Fulbright Commission, the Greater Baltimore Cultural Alliance, the Houghton Library, Johns Hopkins University, the Lannan Foundation, the Lewis Center for the Arts, the MacDowell Colony, the Mid Atlantic Arts Foundation, the Schmuhl family, the Seamus Heaney Centre for Poetry, the Sewanee Writers' Conference, and the Virginia Center for the Creative Arts.

I'm very grateful to Carmine Starnino, Simon Dardick, and everyone at Véhicule Press for giving these poems a home in print.

Thanks finally to the friends who read and responded so thoughtfully to this manuscript—Rebecca Aronson, Caitlin Doyle, Dora Malech, Tomás Morín, Mary Jo Salter, Tess Taylor, David Yezzi—and especially to my first reader, Shannon Robinson.

Signal
EDITIONS

Carmine Starnino, Editor
Michael Harris, Founding Editor

FIRE NEVER SLEEPS Carla Hartsfield
THE RHINO GATE POEMS George Ellenbogen
SHADOW CABINET Richard Sanger
MAP OF DREAMS Ricardo Sternberg
THE NEW WORLD Carmine Starnino
THE LONG COLD GREEN EVENINGS OF SPRING Elisabeth Harvor
KEEP IT ALL Yves Boisvert (Translated by Judith Cowan)
THE GREEN ALEMBIC Louise Fabiani
THE ISLAND IN WINTER Terence Young
A TINKERS' PICNIC Peter Richardson
SARACEN ISLAND: THE POEMS OF ANDREAS KARAVIS David Solway
BEAUTIES ON MAD RIVER: SELECTED AND NEW POEMS Jan Conn
WIND AND ROOT Brent MacLaine
HISTORIES Andrew Steinmetz
ARABY Eric Ormsby
WORDS THAT WALK IN THE NIGHT Pierre Morency
    (Translated by Lissa Cowan and René Brisebois)
A PICNIC ON ICE: SELECTED POEMS Matthew Sweeney
HELIX: NEW AND SELECTED POEMS John Steffler
HERESIES: THE COMPLETE POEMS OF ANNE WILKINSON, 1924-1961
    Edited by Dean Irvine
CALLING HOME Richard Sanger
FIELDER'S CHOICE Elise Partridge
MERRYBEGOT Mary Dalton
MOUNTAIN TEA Peter Van Toorn
AN ABC OF BELLY WORK Peter Richardson
RUNNING IN PROSPECT CEMETERY Susan Glickman
MIRABEL Pierre Nepveu (Translated by Judith Cowan)
POSTSCRIPT Geoffrey Cook
STANDING WAVE Robert Allen
THERE, THERE Patrick Warner
HOW WE ALL SWIFTLY: THE FIRST SIX BOOKS Don Coles
THE NEW CANON: AN ANTHOLOGY OF CANADIAN POETRY
    Edited by Carmine Starnino
OUT TO DRY IN CAPE BRETON Anita Lahey
RED LEDGER Mary Dalton
REACHING FOR CLEAR David Solway
OX Christopher Patton
THE MECHANICAL BIRD Asa Boxer
SYMPATHY FOR THE COURIERS Peter Richardson
MORNING GOTHIC: NEW AND SELECTED POEMS George Ellenbogen
36 CORNELIAN AVENUE Christopher Wiseman
THE EMPIRE'S MISSING LINKS Walid Bitar
PENNY DREADFUL Shannon Stewart
THE STREAM EXPOSED WITH ALL ITS STONES D.G. Jones
PURE PRODUCT Jason Guriel
ANIMALS OF MY OWN KIND Harry Thurston
BOXING THE COMPASS Richard Greene
CIRCUS Michael Harris
THE CROW'S VOW Susan Briscoe
WHERE WE MIGHT HAVE BEEN Don Coles

Véhicule Press